IN THE LIGHT OF SOL

IN THE LIGHT OF SOL

Warren Sunkar

Copyright © 2017 Warren Sunkar

The moral right of the author has been asserted.

All rights reserved.

No part of this publication may be reproduced, stored in a retrieval system, or transmitted, in any form or by any means, without the prior permission in writing of the publisher, nor be otherwise circulated in any form of binding or cover other than that in which it is published and without a similar condition including this condition being imposed on the subsequent purchaser.

National Library of Australia Cataloguing-in-Publication entry

Creator: Sunkar, Warren, author.

Title: In the light of Sol / Warren Sunkar.

ISBN: 9780995371620 (paperback)

Subjects: Short stories. Poetry. Essays.

Dewey Number: A820.8

Publishing Consultants: Pickawoowoo Publishing Group

(interior & cover layout)

With a dedication to Ian. R. Crane.

And a warm smile to Lisa R.

Foreword

The pieces The Sword, Lost in a Labyrinth, Your Reign Now Ends and A World Rent in Twain, were pieces of prophetic writings given by this author in the year 2010. These writings were to highlight the then coming shift of 2012- 2017 which is fast coming to its end. They are not meant to be taken personally or fearfully and give a small glimmer into the dynamics of much that has been taking place behind the scenes of this period. Please use discernment.

May these writings find their way into the hands of only those who can truly benefit from them.

Warren Sunkar

Contents

Creative Works 1
The Sword 2
Running Back Up the Mountain 6
Lost in a Labyrinth 14
When the Lights Go Out… 19
Your Reign Now Ends 25
Love in a Living Moment 29
We Kept Tripping Over Our Feet. 34
A World Rent in Twain 37
A Waltz to Remember 43
In the Light of Sol 50
Esoteric Articles 53
Shifting Relativities 54
Babel 58
The Brothers of Shadow 65

The God of Illusions 75

False Offerings 86

Pseudo Occultism 91

Positively Confused! 95

The New Age
When "Waking Up" Just Means Deeper Sleep! 103

Primal Shame 110

The Fire of God's Love 114

As the Clouds Break 117

CREATIVE WORKS

THE SWORD

The skies have darkened
The world is shaking
Rising tensions and signs
Of immanent catastrophe
Approaching mankind
Of these days
You have been warned
The dragon is rising
Casting its shadow
Over the world
Coiling around
And constricting the earth
And you all wear its face
A monster with broken wings
Compelled by deficiency
Spurred by hatred
That would try and take flight
And dare to war with God

Breathlessly we watch you

In the Light of Sol

Contract into fear
Civilised savages
With an intellect
And systematic cunning
A New World Order
But a sentence of death
And last stance
Of the damned
A withdrawing tide
Into a darkening wave
Struggling to contain
Its growing fury
Boiling up, stretching out
Trying to block out the sun

Before this we stand
Unmoved and unafraid
Watching and waiting
As you writhe in vehemence
Hissing at the approaching light
Your great roar
But a desperate scream
Of a countless lost
And wailing voices
Your seething hatred
But a hopelessness turned
To lash out
At what you cannot be

Warren Sunkar

Nor understand
A wrath that would
Fall upon us in fury
And tear us to pieces

From within the chaos
Of this fallen world
We have struggled
Through the darkened veil
Disturbed by what we have seen
And what has been awakened
Remembering why we are here
And now the time has come
To lay down this life
And willingly we must submit
To be claimed by an authority
That you do not heed
From a place unseen
For never has this life
Been our own

Now the hand of love outstretched
Must be withdrawn
And clenched into a fist
So does come the Sword
And many shall stand as one
Wielded by a greater hand
Overshadowed by a higher will

In the Light of Sol

Thrust into the darkness
To shatter this matrix
Of illusion and desire
And drive the darkness
Back under the seal
And all that you have built
Shall fall apart
And all that you hold
Shall be taken away
Blinded by ignorance
Complacent in arrogance
Unprepared you will be
Forced to confront
A reality denied
Yet reside within
Exposed and naked
Cringing in fear
Forced to awaken
From the curse
Of a darkened sleep
Rendered to your knees
Before the Lord
You shall wonder
And you shall weep

RUNNING BACK UP THE MOUNTAIN

The golden rays of the Great Central Suns permeated all of God's creation.

Within the temple of Love and sitting by the side of his smiling master, Anura (whose name means regal heart) held alignment with the Source of All. Absorbed in infinite wonder, his golden robe of light shimmered fantastically as together they meditated on top of the Holy Mountain.

Here, Life's blessings were dispensed throughout the worlds.

One day as they were immersed in the great effulgence of cosmos, a strange murmuring arose from the valley below and upon hearing it Anura became distracted. As he attuned to these odd and discordant sounds he heard the cries and pains of many suffering beings and was disturbed as he pondered upon the chaos far below.

His master, sensing his disciple's distraction asked,

"What ails you my son?"

Anura answered, "Master, this moment I find it hard to hold my alignment. As the cries of those in the valley meet my ears, it disturbs my being to know there is such suffering in those people upon the Earth."

"Oh them!" his master chuckled.

"What do you mean?" asked Anura.

His master looked at him and replied, "They are all suffering from a little lunacy."

His teacher then went cross-eyed and swirled a finger around his ear!

But his disciple did not understand this well intentioned candour and just frowned all the harder. Sometimes he did not understand his master's sense of humour.

His radiant master looked at him fondly and spoke.

"Here upon the mountain, we bring life to all of God's creation. If we neglect our duty then other worlds might suffer. Should those of the Earth seek their way out of the valley then nothing can truly stop them. They need only brave the mountain and thus we wait here to receive them."

"But master, no one comes!" Anura replied very seriously.

"It seems their cries are growing more desperate and I think it better if I went down to assist them. I will teach the way up the mountain to God. Nothing can deter me!"

The master looked into the eyes of his serious and

grave disciple and he knew that look.

"I see you have made a choice and I know that nothing I can say will dissuade thee."

His teacher then stood up and walked over to a dimensional doorway on their left labelled The Shadowlands and said: "The ways of this world are treacherous and dark, if the people see your radiance they will kill you. You will need to leave your golden robe here my son and put on worldly garb. Here in the holy temple I shall keep your golden robe and watch over thee."

Excited at the thought of helping humanity, Anura stripped off and put on a worldly robe. It had once been his master's robe long ago and had been saved for such an occasion. It was dull, colourless and very heavy but he would not let that deter him.

"God bless!" his master said as he opened the door.

Barely acknowledging his master, Anura did not see the tearful glint in his teacher's deep and knowing eyes, and with great enthusiasm and excitement he disappeared through the doorway to descend the mountain.

As he ran down the steep ravine he was so enthralled by his mission he hardly noticed the skies darkening with each step he took.

He pressed on down the mountain.

As Anura drew closer to the valley the air had become heavier and more polluted. The ethers felt lifeless and dense, and in a short while he realised he could no longer see the sun. He hesitated for a moment as the strange sensation of fear pulsed through him but he pressed on because he would not let that deter him.

Then as Anura entered the Earth, strange sounds hurt his sensitive ears and there was an awful smell.

As he looked around he beheld many strange things.

Grey concrete monoliths towered over him through a polluted haze. Automobiles roared and beeped, unnatural lights flashed about him.

He paused to catch his breath. He felt queasy because the moon above him made him feel quite sick and disoriented.

Everywhere it was very busy and noisy and what was even stranger was Earth's humanity!

No one noticed him or each other. People would just walk by in a strange hypnotic trance. Their smiles had no joy; their movements were discordant with life. Their eyes seemed vacant and they looked very sick yet they kept going about their business as if nothing was wrong.

Yes… Anura thought. Things were very strange down here!

He became confused and a little fearful because he did not know what to do.

Yet the fire of enthusiasm burned in his heart and he would have nothing deter him!

So he decided to stay for a while, trying to learn their language in a hope to communicate with the people.

He went to their schools of education and philosophy, watched their strange televisions and even frequented their very popular cafes. Yet over time, all this only confused him more because though they chattered a lot, they didn't seem to know what they were chattering about.

Their words were all nonsensical.

He felt a little sad and frustrated. So in an attempt to connect with Earth's humanity, he thought to imitate them for a while and began walking around in circles, smiling to them as if nothing was wrong.

In a short time the moon overhead began to completely disorient him. The heavy and polluted atmosphere began to make him tired and before long he fell asleep. In a strange state of dreaming he wandered around aimlessly with them.

Lost in this dreaming world, everyone was anxious and confused. The people did not realise they were asleep and they often argued with each other.

No one seemed to notice the strange black shadows that whispered incessantly into everyone's ear.

What was very strange was that everyone liked to wear heavy chains. In this dismal place the bigger the chains one had, the greater the social status. Some people wore chains so large and heavy that they could not move.

It was very surreal because everyone struggled so intensely under their burdens yet no one wanted to get rid of them. This was because in this dream world, great chains were high-class fashion and everyone that wore them thought themselves a king!

In the Light of Sol

Everyone was quite crazy.

People wailed and howled, others cried or laughed manically as they worked so hard to get nowhere. Confusion pervaded everything and nothing made any sense. Everything was upside down and inside out.

It was complete lunacy!

Anura started to be overwhelmed with fear.

Then suddenly something fell from above and landed upon Anura's head, snapping him awake. He rubbed his sore head as he picked up a small stone. It was polished and its surfaces were reflective as a mirror. When he looked into it, catching a glint of light through the dark clouds above, he saw the smiling face of his beloved master and some words flashed through his mind… WAKE UP!

He looked around and wondered how long had he been asleep.

It seemed like lifetimes.

He remembered his divine mission – now nothing could deter him!

"Wake up!" He called to the people that walked about him.

But only a few of the people stirred and most of them just grumbled. They continued to go about their selfish business, bumping into each other, chattering incessantly and poisoning the Earth. They were all lost to their darkened dreaming.

Inspired, he thought to show them a better way.

So while they laboriously worked on meaningless things, he danced and sang before them.

They tried to ignore him.

As they bumped into and hurt each other, he would pick them up and heal them.

Yet they resented him.

He spoke to them about a Love that knows no bounds.

They grew suspicious.

Because he would not let them sleep, they grew angry.

Restless and disturbed in their slumber they began to circle Anura. Snarling, gossiping and threatening, he could hear the shadows in their dream world, whispering.

When Anura said he knew God, raising the mirror his master had given him to catch a small glint of light from the Great Divine Sun, they fell back, dazzled and confused. They called him evil; taking up their pitchforks and burning torches they attacked. Coming at him with a collective roar, they grabbed at his clothes and tore them off but Anura was light and swift of foot and jumped over them.

Naked, he took flight out of the valley. Like a comet, he tore up the side of the mountain as fast as his legs could carry him and nothing could deter him!

Nude and a little scared but with a sigh of relief he burst through the door into the master's temple. Panting and exhausted he looked up to see his master standing there with an expectant smile, holding his golden robes for him. Anura put them back on.

"What did you learn on Earth?" asked his master as together they sat down for a new planetary alignment.

Anura spoke thoughtfully, "One can offer the keys of Life but they will not free those who love their chains…"

His master smiled, "Anything else?"

Anura added. "Yeah! Before we can teach them about God…those guys will first need to learn a better sense of humour!"

(Anura went cross-eyed and swirled his finger.)

They gazed at each other fondly and chuckled intensely.

It was good to be home.

LOST IN A LABYRINTH

Lost in a labyrinth
Its walls closing in
Vexation and distraction
Your attention diverted
In countless directions
Chasing temporal glitter
Your personal life force
Leeched and harvested
Within the confines
Of this vibratory prison
For this world
Of time and space
Is but a measure and quantity
Of self-delusion
Manipulated and manufactured
Keeping you in ignorance
In which you are
Dogs chasing their tails
Running a gauntlet
Of dualistic striving

Watching you, we shudder
Shutting down
Closing up
Consuming yourselves
In Identification
With the condensation
Of this illusive
And apparent reality
That closes over you
As do the jaws
Of a steel trap
A matrix of collective mind
Enforcing itself in denial
Impressing individual subconscious
Attempting to sustain
It's dying self
With great sadness
We see that humanity
Has been taken captive
Upon a rudderless ship
Drifting to oblivion

Your societies and peoples
Swell and stir
Struggling to process
A plethora of ideas and ideals
As you swing
Upon a pendulum

Warren Sunkar

Of antithesis and alternation
Trying to escape
What will come to pass
Feebly trying to resuscitate
Old and various
Codes and moralities
In a final effort
To save yourselves
While falling away
Into greater disgrace
Which in the face
Of new life
Acquaints to insanity
That leaves you all
To a complete rupture
With truth
Which to us is but refuse
That has been discarded

Woe to you humanity
Such wrath have you
Brought upon yourselves
And this heart weeps
At your blindness
For you have
Turned your backs
On truth
Compromised your hearts

And heeded not
Our warnings
The children of God
Lay discarded
In the streets
Destitute and abandoned
Their testimony ignored
Their gifts rejected
And you laugh at them
With a devil's delight
Now behold
The tide does turn
The lion descends
Upon the world
And he shall snatch you
Off your feet
Bear you to the ground
And tear your throats out
And the world will
Thunder and quake
At his coming

Take heed
Brothers and Sisters
The final call resounds
The harvest shall be gathered
And the roar of truth
Shall echo throughout the valley

Warren Sunkar

Confusions and rumours
Shall abound
As many begin to sense
The great and immanent shift
Realising with great pain
And distress
A failed opportunity
For now with great speed
Shall this world be quickened
And you have all
Been caught sleeping
And to you
Who count yourselves
Amongst the living
Make haste, come forth
And present yourselves
Lest you be lost forever
For it is time
That the children of Love
Find their place
As this world
Shall now be forced
To stare its death
In its face

May your courage
Be found in Christ
And may your offering
Be worthy…

WHEN THE LIGHTS GO OUT…

It was night and the rain poured down heavily outside. Thunder shook the heavens as an electrical storm brought down the rage of the winds damaging the city's energy grid. The lights went out and we sat in darkness.

I lit a candle on a small table in the living room.

My friend Monique sat next to me in a reclining chair, she was greatly saddened by what was revealing itself in the world as we both pondered the powerful and often disturbing revelations of the times we lived in. Rumours were surfacing about the elite and ruling class of the world, with evidence emerging of horrors and acts of hidden depravity, of child trafficking, ritual sacrifice and cannibalism.

It was an auspicious moment to share insight into such things.

She looked at me in despair, "Is it true?"

I met her look in the flickering candle light.

"The wealthy and powerful over generations of miscreant rule, long ago lost themselves to involuntary magic and thus to madness. I can assure you that what you are hearing is only the smallest part."

She sat, thoughtful. "Is this why we are being attacked in our own homes and in every aspect of our lives? Through our televisions, radios and computers it feels as though we are being hypnotised and programmed to accept their culture of death. The more I investigate it seems every facet of society has been infiltrated. People are so lost and confused, programmed into believing the lies and false narratives given them. Fear has overridden their sanity and often they turn on each other. I know we cannot trust anything that the media says anymore."

"Yes," I said, "it has all been infiltrated and much goes on behind closed doors. As this world awakens, the family of dark seek to keep humanity chained and powerless. Those of the shadows have merged with alien means, using all means at their disposal to subvert and capture humanity dragging them into their advancing technocratic hell."

Thunder rumbled outside, shadows flickered on the wall from the dim candlelight that cast an eerie glow.

There was such sadness in her eyes. "Where did it all go so wrong?"

I replied, "There are entities that exist in spheres that are sealed from human awareness yet if we are not vigilant as a race, they can rise and consume us. When we venerate the material over our inner spirit and become too selfishly inclined, we can fall victim to beings that exist in realms beyond the threshold not meant for us. It is to these the elite make their sacrificial oblations."

Her voice broke in angrily. "We need to run them down and make them pay for their crimes!"

"Yes, these things are now to be brought to an end," I replied dispassionately.

"However, in this convoluted world the line between perpetrator and victim are not so easily drawn. I can assure you that many have sought in humanity's past to run down such evil, never seeming to catch it. Falling even deeper into their illusions, many of the so-called righteous became what they themselves had reviled. Before we lose ourselves to hatred and condemnation we must first see how we feed this very evil around us."

"What do you mean?" she asked with a confused look.

I met her look. "I call on you to look within and see the murderer, liar and thief inside yourself!"

She stared at me, shocked by my words.

I kept speaking.

"Look around, do you think yourself so innocent?

"We have sold our brothers and sisters of humanity to a slave culture in want for material luxury. We have turned our backs on the raping of the Earth. With the words that you speak and the decisions you make, what have you been in consent with?"

Seeing her confusion, I continued.

"This act of planetary transmutation must come from within. We must see how we ourselves participate in this matrix of death and take back our sense of deeper responsibility. It will be hard because these late generations have seen humanity revelling in great selfishness and denial.

"Know that before we can even see the true solution, we must first face our own shadows!"

Tears welled up in her eyes, "It is all so confusing."

She looked at me a little angry and rejecting. "It seems you would make us vulnerable. In a time of madness you would have us give up our self-defence. You are scaring me…"

I replied, "In Truth the deeper problems of this world are now way beyond human capacity to deal with. There are great divine energies and beings that have been drawn to Earth at this time of planetary change. We are called to align with the new energies entering the Earth, with them lie our healing and true protection. In holding this alignment the filth of the world is being brought to the surface to be cleared. We are being called to become conduits of such energy."

She questioned, "How can one know what you say is true?"

"You seek a security for yourself that I cannot give," I replied. In times of darkness you cannot rely on the outer senses; and do you think in trying to cling to your illusions you are safer?

"Now it is time to face your fears."

I leaned toward the table and blew out the candle.

We sat in the silence letting her ponder deeply on what I had said. I felt confusion and resistances arise in her mind and felt her fear at what was being revealed.

My voice sounded in the darkness, "If you look out, you will only succumb to darkness and confusion. How can you defend yourself when the enemy is seemingly everywhere?

"You have a deeper light," I continued, "that can see through the illusions of this world but you must be willing to seek the truth and find your true centre. Know that when the lights go out, if you let go of fear, the real can awaken…"

I could feel her intense struggle.

Thunder boomed, the rain poured harder. Trees thrashed in the wind. The world outside seemed like it was destroying itself.

My voice echoed, "We must overcome this evil not by looking outside of ourselves but by first looking within."

I could feel her turmoil, she wanted to run away but in the darkness there was nowhere to run and in the blackness of this night there was nothing to grasp for comfort. Alone and in the dark she was forced to sit with her madness and fear. I felt her panic and despair because here there was no one to attack or to blame.

She broke out into a deep sobbing.

I remained silent and a long time passed. There, in the deep silence of the long dark moment, she eventually let go. Facing her self-delusion and madness, having seen the deeper truth, she gave up her fear.

Together in the pitch blackness we relaxed in the storm and breathed deeply, at one with the night. Within my being the dark light of the spirit seed pulsed softly in electric light.

There Monique opened the eye of her deep intuition piercing the shadows and darkness.

"I feel that we should not be hypnotised by the lies and illusions the family of dark have cast before us," she said. "All this technocratic sorcery is but a psychological trick…they have used us to build our own prison cells. It is we in our fear who have given them substance and power over us."

"Yes," I said, "that is why we are asked to let go of this world of illusions, do you understand?"

"Yes." In a strong impersonal voice she spoke the words; "It is the world of the personality that is the illusion. We are called to take leave of this madness."

I asked: "What do you see?"

"I can see that their time is done!" her voiced boomed.

Then lightning flashed and thunder cracked all around us…

YOUR REIGN NOW ENDS

Oh wayward brother
Your hands are stained red
And you hide them
Behind your back
Your legacy of generations
Flows as a river of blood
And now at its end
Shall you drown
In your own filth
Adorned in robes
Lined with stolen jewels
That sparkle lacklustre
As do the stars
In Lucifer's firmament
Do you bow your heads
Before a reverted cross
Servants of death
Commanders of the hordes
The very cancer
Consuming this planet

Warren Sunkar

You who know nothing
You who hear nothing
Except the sound
Of your own loud voices
Whence do you think
Your salvation comes?
Clinging to images
Of saints and saviours
Long departed
You pray only to shadows
Know your phantoms
Cannot save you
And from whence comes
Your authority?
Burnt offerings
And empty speeches
Only pollute the ethers
Expounding your corruption
Revealing your lack
Of true acquaintance
For your rites and ceremonies
Have been reduced
To a failing sorcery
Enslaving the weak
Through aeonic manipulation
Imitators and adulterers
Know your father
Is a liar

In the Light of Sol

Now take heed
Oh poisoned priests
The destiny
Of the ages is nigh
And the sword of right
Shall be dipped
Into this pool of stagnancy
For no longer
Shall your rest
Be found in its arrogance
And you shall tremble
Before the thunder
That comes
And it is given us
To torture your hearts
With the word of life
And trample your death
Under our feet
And you will revile
Making war with us
Yet we the children
Of Life
Shall laugh in your face
For do you think this world
Means anything to us
Know you may slay the image
But not the Life
For it lies
Beyond your reach

Warren Sunkar

And before the light
Of the living Christ
You shall see
The darkness and death
That is self
And you shall howl
And lament
Over the falsehood
And madness
You have wrought
For we shall overcome
And in dispersing desperation
We see that you shall
Cling to your idols
In shame and in dread
But all is in vain…
For "Our Father"
Is of the living
And heeds not
The dead

Your reign ends now

LOVE IN A LIVING MOMENT

Dust particles danced in the light of the sunlit window. My friend smiled as I walked into the room.

That week there had been a steady precipitation of higher energies and currents which had brought a subtle change of direction to an awakening experience we had been unfolding into.

It was a soft call of the soul that had called us together.

Life energies gently surged through my being and her beautiful eyes sparkled with a receptive shine. There was no need to speak because everything was seen in the living moment.

We drew close as she looked into my eyes with such purity of being that my heart opened and rejoiced as I met her beautiful gaze.

Gently touching her face, subtle electric currents flickered between us in a soft transmission of love. Safe and relaxed in each other's presence, we had nothing to hide from one another.

My spirit was tenderly stirred as she opened her being to me as a soft song of love played upon the ethers. Playfully we smiled to each other as we began to undress.

With a glance she beckoned me to the other room and I followed. I picked up a small candle and matches from the sunlit window sill as we went.

We then sat cross-legged on the floor, naked and unabashed before each other.

A light and beautiful energy washed through the room as we looked into each other's eyes. I lit the small candle and placed it next to us as we shut our eyes to give thanks to the Divine Mother. Her gentle and pervasive presence blessed the room. With soft ethereal whispers of light, we could feel protective gentle spirits dance into the room.

The ritual was sweet and touching yet it was our openness to life that evoked the living spirit to play with us.

As we came back to meet each other's gaze. I gently brought her on top of me as she wrapped her legs around my body. I did not enter inside her. There were no expectations or attachments, just the beating of our hearts and the offering of ourselves to God.

Together we embraced with a delicate kiss.

Slowly, rhythmically we harmonised our breathing, inhaling and exhaling as we let go of our surroundings. Unfolding yet simultaneously merging, we gently collapsed into a still point that lifted us both into resonance with the cosmic breath.

Our breathing gradually went deeper as we gently clasped each other's bodies though almost unconscious of doing so. Together, we slowly looked up in unison, releasing into a realm beyond time and space, losing the relativity of our body consciousness.

Allowing the breathing to rise in a crescendo, lifting our energies higher through our bodies, we let them collapse in unison. As *one* our energy fields opened in delight, unfolding as a cosmic flower.

Beautiful living light gently radiated from above. We raised our hearts to meet this sensuous space as the energy flowed down, fluid and delightful.

Our bodies began to pulsate, her legs wrapped tighter around my torso and she rubbed firmly against my body. Our subtle bodies pulsed as one, the energies of life swirled around us in a vortex of colour and I felt a glow of energy lift from my base washing upward through us to meet the downward flowing energies pouring through our crown in a splashing of soothing ecstasy.

My mind's eye opened as we were transported into a cosmic rapture. We started to dissolve in a suspension of time as we were lifted high into the exquisite love of the Cosmic Mother. Flowing, glowing and spinning in a thrilling dance of unspeakable bliss. Divine spirits of Life crowned us in a euphoric dream as light pulsed though us in a joyous wave.

I felt the throbbing of my physical body somewhere far below. Then in a pleasing orgasmic surge of energy which released through my heart, I felt the powerful rush of liquid light through me…

It released.

In a timeless peak we dissipated into nothing and everything.

As we drifted down back into our bodies, we exhaled deeply as we softly collapsed into each other physically. Sweat glistened over our skin in the soft candle light. Then slowly as we met each other's eyes in such joyous acknowledgement, we expelled our breath which released us into a deep relaxation as we gently fell backwards to lay on the floor. Her legs still wrapped around me as her naked arched body found the soft rug.

Then, deeply inhaling and exhaling we let go and released the experience as we lay there in silence.

There a long, sweet and euphoric moment passed, we were regenerated and thrilled. Smiling in elation and wonder as the divine energies very slowly and tenderly dissipated…

Hours later…I sat bare chested on the balcony taking in the sweet smelling rose that was in my hand. My friend was still naked and looking out over the world. The warm rays of the sun illuminated her naked body.

She spoke as she pondered, "It makes you wonder what people are doing, they have forgotten so much!" She looked at me with a loving smile watching me smell the rose.

"The true tantra is the dance with Life. It is you communing with that rose, it is me dancing with the rays of father sun, it is us opening to God. What people are forgetting is that every moment is a living moment…" she spun around in a pirouette to face me.

I looked at her fondly. She was radiant.

"In this world people think it is another that gives them happiness and so they take it from each other. They have forgotten the blessing of pure Life that would dance in their hearts if only they would stop clinging so hard to that which is confusing them. True sex has always been a divine communion."

She replied, "It's so crazy isn't it, all this debased love only leads to pain and so much misunderstanding. How did our world get so twisted? I feel like shouting to everyone just wake up…what are you doing?"

I laughed. "They would look at us as if we were the idiots. Perhaps they are not ready?"

She looked at me with a beautiful smile.

"Well, they are the idiots because they don't know what they are missing!"

She jumped into my arms and we broke into laughter.

WE KEPT TRIPPING OVER OUR FEET...

Sitting in a corner of confusion and fear,
Afraid of our own shadow.
You looked down and took pity on me,
Seeing my well intentions,
Yet marvelling at my stupidity.
A mother's love is what is needed for a wounded child,
And we have been a belligerent race,
Often cruel and wild.

I know the days of darkness are over,
Your healing has come.
Soothing this broken heart
Bringing everything undone.
Helping us to let go of our madness and fear
Letting us know "our war" is already won!

You are a conundrum to this wayward mind,
The awakening flame of this heart.

In the Light of Sol

Please forgive the times I could not see you,
We have been foolish and are still learning.
Now I know in your forgiving presence
For what I had been yearning…
We have been so caught up in ourselves,
Denying your life giving kiss.
How foolish have we been
Not knowing such universal bliss.
As our ancient eye now opens, let us see
Our greatest joy comes from divine purity.

Oh great feminine
May we have the honour of this cosmic dance?
But may you lead for we have forgotten…
Turning, spinning, keeping the inner galaxies moving
I look forward to this infinity of grooving.
May I never seek to hold my sisters to me
But lift them to the greater sky
That they may tell me the things
I cannot see,
For often us males are so blind
So caught up in self and mind.

Oh, women do not bear our burdens,
You honour us in being what you are.
If you dance fearless,
We shall honour you,
And in our joy dance fearless too.

Warren Sunkar

Thank God this age is done!
As the skies open
Let's have some fun,
It's time to forget this male egoic prance.
Beautiful Cosmic woman,
Please teach us idiots, how to dance…

A WORLD RENT IN TWAIN

A world rent in twain
Its people caged and herded
Drawn into a vortex
Of an impulse inverted
A sea of flailing arms
And terrified faces
Clawing at each other
Trying to gain height
Whilst upside down
And standing upon
One another
Slaves of the great wheel
Chained to the powers
That keeps them
Their sustenance drawn
From the ethers of death
In an undivine symbiosis
With their dying host
The prince of darkness
And his incorporeal children

Warren Sunkar

The shadows of the outer ring
Such is the horror and misery
Of they who do not live
But are lived
Such are the children
Of this world

And your mocking laughter
Resounds around us
Condemning us as fools
Judging us
As you have served yourselves
Your verdict has been hard
And we have been forced to hide
As we struggled to love
And battled to truth
Enduring and persevering
Through the filth
Of this sewer
Within the confines
Of a twisted social morality
For this world has become
A den of beggars and thieves
Of vampires, druk and druja
Set upon themselves
Refusing to let go
To what they have stolen
Fiends that would savour

In the Light of Sol

This dying world
Sustaining its lie
And its pain
And will fight to the end
As it aborts itself
Keeping themselves trapped
Within a curse

Your army is gathering
And the masks that you wear
Feign the misleading truth
Of your collective intention
Drawn from all corners and beliefs
Uniting in desperation
Waving a banner
Of false righteousness
Surging with fear
Agitated into a frenzy
By ethereal necrophagi
And under the spell
Of a counterfeit spirit
Courage enraged by cowardice
Is but panic
Inspired by fear
And your so-called virtue
That you claim
Is but evil and hypocrisy
Driven into a fanaticism

Warren Sunkar

Into a united charge
Against the living
So shall life cast you back
And throw you from the earth

The storm is coming
Judgement is at hand
Armageddon is here
With trembling hearts
Now, do you begin to stir
In the realisation
That your lives are amiss
And that something is going
Terribly wrong
In the face of impending doom
We ask you
How would you save
That which is already dead?
And we shake our heads
As we watch you
Rise in self-adoration
Crying for unity and solidarity
Which are but the cries
Of the fearful
Backed into a corner
Trying to raise up the lifeless
And you will shout your slogans
Of truth, love and liberation

In the Light of Sol

Practical idealists
With doctrines of peace
But you are prostitutes of life
As you set about to war
With the very cause
That came to redeem you
For now the most deceptive
And cunning of murderers
Shall wear a humanitarian face

Wake up swine
And face your self-deception
Herein lies your charge
And your final chance
For time has already left
And you will see
An imitation of life
And spiritual bankruptcy
In collective bondage
And united misery
Whose number and name
Is legion
For your governments are failing
Your leaders are trembling
And your systems are falling apart
As you huddle for safety
And rally for order
So shall you receive your mark

Warren Sunkar

Out of control, spiralling down
With nothing to hold
Swept away
By the dark reaper's scythe
Caught in a net
Shall you be dragged
To the depths
Wailing for true light

A WALTZ TO REMEMBER

On a night of a full moon, gentle spirits were beckoning me to a familiar rock on a small hill that sat overlooking lush fields of a nearby valley. It was upon this rock that I often found solace to sit and contemplate.

As I walked up the hill, the night sky glittered brilliantly.

The moon's silvery white light lit up a path before me, bathing the trees around me in its soft luminescence. The night was still and mystical.

Reaching the top of the hill, I noticed the glow of a small fire on the rock and a shadowed figure sitting silently, staring out into the night sky.

I approached quietly to see an elderly woman wrapped in a light shawl. Her black hair was streaked with silver that seemed to reflect the very starlight sparkling above us. I did not know her ethnicity but glancing at her, it seemed she might have come from any one of the tribes of Earth. There in the moonlight I silently mused, because it felt she might just be all of them.

Her deep black eyes looked out into space. She was unmoved by my approach.

I invited myself to sit next to her so that I could share the glorious view of the star filled firmament.

"Dear old mother," I said, "what brings you here this night?"

She turned and looked deeply into my eyes. There was an unfathomable depth in her stare. Though she wore the body of an elderly woman, I was in the aura of a powerful spirit.

I stared back at her wonderingly. I was trying to feel out who or what she was when a voice whispered on the breeze…the Great Grandmother.

A long moment passed. Her presence felt as ancient as the moon.

"I'm not that old," she said eventually. I knew she was reading my mind. She smiled playfully, and then gave me a flirtatious wink!

I smiled back bashfully. Her deep eyes sparkled as spiritedly as a young child's yet her poise commanded respect as her strong presence overshadowed her aged appearance.

I wondered what was to become of this strange auspicious night. Why had I been led here?

"My dear boy, my sweet child, take my hand," she said in answer to my thought.

She opened her weathered hand, which I softly took in mine.

There on the hilltop we both shut our eyes.

I was released into a vision of dreaming. I watched the

skies turn quickly, rotating from night to day. I observed the Earth's seasons change in a visual collage of timelessness. I saw continents shift, forests grow and seas change in a flowing graphic of beauty that was played in my mind's eye.

I felt light and buoyant. The vision kept going as I watched in awe.

I saw the journey of humanity throughout the ages. Witnessing the rise and fall of great civilisations and strange things to behold. I observed alien realities manipulating the human race and realised that humanity's long history was far different from what anyone of this modern age could perceive.

The Grandmother Spirit had been there through it all.

As I contemplated what I had just seen, the vision shifted.

I became a little girl walking through a field of flowers remembering the ethereal innocence of a young child as I ran, danced and played.

Upon a storyboard of a feminine life playing out before me, I quickly shifted in years. I became a young teenager staring out under the stars, yearning for love. I felt a young girl's beautiful dreams and high aspirations.

The vision kept going…

I was a young woman finding her first lover…then felt the tears of first heartbreak, the confusion and pain. I felt courage return and a new love come. I watched the struggles and dramas of an earthly life. Experiencing the birth of my first child, watching my children grow with love and seeing them leave with heartache. I witnessed my life change and my husband grow old in an incessant visual stream of joy and sadness, heartbreak and hope. I felt the cruel touch of time, the ageing of my body.

The tone of the vision shifted again. It became faster…

I felt the loss of loved ones, loneliness and despair. I saw young men recklessly run off to war…images of horror, violence and brutality. I felt the worry of mothers for their children, the yearning of wives hoping for their partners to return; the Earth being destroyed. The madness of the modern world swirled around me in a vortex of painful imagery of hopelessness and anguish. It kept going; the vision had become almost frantic.

I reeled and let go of the Great Grandmother's hand to stop the vision.

I felt the Grandmother's pain, there was a tear rolling down her cheek.

"I have known many ages…and none has been so strange as this one," she said.

With a look I questioned her.

I felt the shame.

She looked into my eyes and read my heart. Her face softened and she said in gentle recognition, "I see you and I are not so different."

She was gazing into my being, tracing the lines of incarnations and cosmic pre-Earth journeys.

I knew what she meant.

The rise and fall of the great civilisations of Earth are nothing but faint ripples upon the ocean of life. The lifetimes of men are but a bauble in space, and all will vanish into nothing but distant memories in the shadows of time.

And what would become of this wayward world?

The glories of so-called modern man are but dust. The vain and the powerful are destined to become but forgotten ghosts. This world civilisation is a towering monument of its disgrace, and here at its end nothing of this age would be left standing. Thus already inscribed upon the ethers was the sad epitaph of this Yuga.

And those of the deep silence had waited patiently throughout it all, watching and calling to humanity to understand and change its ways.

I smiled with a sad knowing and we held each other's gaze in the quietness.

There I pondered for many moments at the strange and wonderful events of this enchanting night.

The breeze had stilled, and it was then that a thought came to my mind. I rose to my feet.

Inspired, I held out my hand, bowing in a time forgotten chivalry.

Now it was she who stared at me questioningly and wonderingly. I smiled.

Curious, she stood up, taking my hand.

As I brought her to my chest I shared a dreaming

of joy, hope and nobility. She looked down at herself, she had become young again. Looking into her eyes I shared a vision of a man looking into the eyes of his first love and together we embraced as we swayed gently together under the stars. We dreamed the healing of the Earth and a new humanity born into an age of wonder, and there we danced through the ages…

After a long and beautiful interlude we gently let go and released.

"Thank you sweet child," she whispered affectionately.

She leant forward and softly kissed my forehead then turned back to stare out over the moonlit valley.

She smiled as she spoke. "Now comes the Great Shift of seasons, the one I have waited for all my long years." There was a sense of expectation and joy in her voice.

We shared the silence staring out to the stars. As the night wore on, sleep began to come over me and my eyes grew heavy. The last vision I had of the Grandmother Spirit was her glowing silver white and then everything faded into darkness.

I awoke as the first rays of the dawning sun broke through the skies. The fire had become whispers of smoke and she had gone.

Standing up to look over the beautiful sunlit valley, I felt strong and rejuvenated.

A whisper entered my mind and I heard her voice – 'Grandma has given you a bath!'

I knew I had received a beautiful healing.

I giggled to myself…at such a strange and beautiful night.

It was one I would never forget…

Months later, I was walking through a busy urban street in a major city. Unnoticed by the people rushing about was an old woman struggling with some shopping bags, trying to navigate the great current of city madness that was all around her. She had tripped up and no one seemed to care.

I walked up to her and offered my hand. She looked up and behind her eyes I saw a familiar glitter.

"My sweet child," the old lady said and gave me a playful wink.

I helped her to her feet and took her bags.

Together we walked through the urban indifference, smiling.

IN THE LIGHT OF SOL

Standing upon a hillside, the faint glow of Love christens the dawning horizon.

Silence, the womb of subtle expectation as nature holds its breath for this moment…

The first ray of light breaks upon the horizon releasing a wave of subtle love that washes all before it. A kookaburra breaks into laughter and in sweet symphony nature comes alive in chorus.

The sun's ray sweeps through my being in a gentle rush of bliss and I have become transparent in its light. I breathe deeply, the liquid plasm of Sol runs through my bodies, lighting and activating the Krystal temple of the brain. My heart has become a diamond absorbing and sharing the living rays of cosmic Light.

I attune my breath; harmonising with the Earth and cosmos. Plasma accretes through me as I bathe in ecstatic bliss, igniting the divine chalice of fire as the warm elixir of delicious liquid light washes through my being.

Truly the new day is here…

In the Light of Sol

The golden sun peaks over the horizon as more light sweeps the sky.

Would you believe that the living sun speaks to those raised to its consciousness? It shares its love with those who would partake in the uninhibited dance of Life. It whispers that the great change is here and my body pulsates in relief as its love softly penetrates my being, washing clear those obstructive energies in the liquid warmth of soft flowing ecstasy.

Nature is now singing her joy. Through my being I channel the subtle currents of New Life, they permeate the Earth and she receives them in love, clearing and bathing her in cosmic love.

Now I turn inward…overflowing with divine joy into the heart of a sleeping humanity.

My whispers of love permeate their dreams… "Awaken children of light, the day is now here.

"Release from the night and leave the momentum of your subconscious dreaming. I am the voice of One calling you through the clouds of yesterday's fancy that keeps you slumbering in the lower substrate."

The light of Sol now breaks through their inner worlds and I rejoice, as the children of Love gently stir in their beds with smiles upon their faces.

The Great Mother kisses softly their cheeks.

They know the time is now…

ESOTERIC ARTICLES

SHIFTING RELATIVITIES

It is obvious that we are living in a time of great change and planetary upheaval. Incoming cosmic energies are bringing with them new life encodings that are greatly affecting planetary life. Today we live in a world of shifting relativities and humanity is called to quickly free itself of its delusions and misconceptions that no longer serve an awakening race.

The revealing quality of these new energies is bringing to the foreground of human consciousness hidden agendas of control and multidimensional interference. This will be a difficult period for much of humanity who have disregarded the many warnings given and not suitably prepared themselves for this period of planetary transitioning.

Simultaneously, however, under stimulation of these new life energies, larger portions of humanity are also recalling their divine and multidimensional lineages. Today, many are witnessing the emergence of those divine beings that are here to assist the planet through its time of radical transformation – an event today understood as the Second Coming.

As the old paradigm collapses people will realise that humanity has been running on subconscious programmes and agreements that have been socially engineered or self-created to shape how they have viewed their reality. Rather than letting go of what is obviously killing them – in their growing fear people mostly deny other alternatives or possibilities that don't affirm their familiarised belief patterns and programmes – they often attack those persons or groups that threaten their delusive realities. As the world becomes more unpredictable, reactive potentialities and situations might get worse.

People should understand that it is the world of the personality that is illusive, and identification with it is causing so much pain and drama. In the rising chaos of our fast changing realities, it is easy to see how people can clutch at old survival tools in terms of egoic belief structures. People today are being socially engineered to a constant state of survival as the world ego seeks by whatever means to adapt and integrate any mechanism, belief or system that may affirm or prolong its deceptive and illusive reality. This includes threatening or killing those people and groups that don't!

However, we are now called to fast let go of the dying, old world paradigm.

In a world of false narratives and delusive programmes it is important to realise that before we are able to truly comprehend the nature of these ongoing and intensive planetary changes, we must first come to discern the true planetary situation as well as the delusive platforms upon which humanity derives much of its "understanding".

Many people are realising that the media are certainly not to be relied on for imparting the truth of the times!

Here we must go beyond superficial measures of inquiry and understand the deeper causative realities that are present beyond what is a materialistically bound, human consciousness spectrum. This could be very confusing and frightening for some but necessary if we are to work consciously through this transition. Know where there is purity of motive, humanity's guides are ever present. However, as the planetary tempo is raised, this will also require greater discernment, sincerity and conscious participation than what has been required in the past, lest humanity falls deeper into the deceptive hands of those exploiters of the race!

Many people understand that we cannot keep living in the manner that we do. Yet so many have been in denial of the planetary situation which now must shift even as the greater portions of the race are still resisting.

It is important to comprehend that beyond the sight of a weary and frightened humanity, the new is arriving. As the world structure collapses it is imperative to shift into a deeper perspective of events.

For those astute and selfless of the race this period

offers incredible opportunities of transformation and true divine initiation. In a world of shifting relativities humanity is decentralising from a self- centred paradigm to become a God-conscious one. Those people who are selflessly serving the divine plan are today understanding that parallel to a collapsing world system exist transcendent energies and divine beings that are inviting those who can answer, into the *new reality*.

With any shift of identification, what is important is often not so much the accumulation of knowledge but the ability to see and let go of that which is stopping us from transitioning. We need to look within and go deep, seeking Divine Truth, inquiring what we identify with, how we ourselves deal with situations and how we interact with the world. Few people consider before they rush out prematurely -trying to save the world that maybe it is time to be still, to listen and be empty, and allow the new and living reality to reveal its true nature.

Perhaps what is revealing itself is so powerful, beautiful and magical that instead of rushing out and adding to the planetary madness, we will stand as one in awe and reverence of the mysteries of God.

BABEL

Many beings today in the grip of escalating world tension and terminal madness are being forced to repeatedly question the reality in which they find themselves. As they walk through the mire of this world, those who are hearing the call to new life are experiencing the deep troubles, chaos and evil that infect themselves and the planet. Now, as they must struggle against a seemingly overwhelming current of collective human delusion and madness, they see a world in its dying throes. A world that has little tolerance for truth, where the strongest and most dominant egos rule over, and at the expense of, the weak and the vulnerable. A civilisation abstract from nature and home to corporate control and barbarism. A society that has fallen deep into self-absorption, self-gratification and materialism. Many are feeling tremendous pressure and tension as they struggle to awaken in this great and tumultuous time in humanity's collective history, and many are feeling and sensing within their hearts that something is going terribly wrong. Confusion shall soon abound as people awaken and gaze in great pain and distress as to the true and daunting situation that now faces them. As they begin to see that in this time of worldly sickness, confusion and despair they are being forced into an abyss by those who are taking advantage of their great confusion and vulnerability.

Many of you are becoming aware of the great manipulators of the human race – beings and intelligences of higher perspectives, great power and evil that have been exercising their dominance over humanity. As to the collective agenda and perfidious intent of these beings, most of humanity is oblivious or only partly aware. Many are sensing that this world is under a new order of evil, and many are feeling an overwhelming futility and powerlessness as the darkness upon the Earth is rising and imposing itself on human civilisation.

When we look out into this world we see that human civilisation has fallen deep into its collective self. The vast majority of beings upon the planet live in a totally spiritless state, having been consumed by and absorbed into materialism which is but the identification of a purely phenomenal existence. Those beings that are awakening in this time are understanding the inverted mess that humanity has become, and are becoming all too acquainted with the great pains, traumas and dangers that confront them through this process in these hostile and aberrant conditions within this formidable archonic matrix of death. Collectively, humanity has been drawn into a field of collective illusion that has been occultly generated and cultivated using humanity itself over successive generations under the guidance and manipulation of an intelligent hierarchy of dark masters that today stands at the head of the current new world order that now opens to its full expression.

This world in its current phase is held firmly in the grip of cosmic evil, and in negative orientation mass humanity has become aligned and polarized anti-Christ. Which is the direct inversion of the collective human life field, expressed in our world today as the prevailing consciousness of the collective that sits in positive attraction towards the direct gravitational pull of Saturn. It is the dominating 'I' consciousness into which collective humanity has been intentionally seduced and drawn and few can truly see the sickening contortion and twisting of the collective mind and truly understand that the dominant consciousness of the collective is upside down and inside out!

Within the collective itself is a point of abstraction that dominates mass humanity in its connection and estrangement, consciously manipulating and controlling civilisation through perfidious means and with nefarious intent.

It is this group of dark masters –Comprised of units of consciousness that have completely and successfully inverted their group field in direct opposition of divine will – who act as a conduit at the top of this grand and evil hierarchy of civilisation known to some as the "great eye". Hidden in humanity's shadows, they control, govern and direct the collective to form the climactic, yet very short, phase of evil dominance known today as the new world order.

From within humanity's ranks they have formed a great hierarchy of intelligence to rule via occult means and understanding. Today they control humanity's religious, political and financial institutions, and utilise the military, media and educational systems to indoctrinate, hypnotise and manipulate humanity into their own evil design.

This tower is one great monstrous and organised system which fallen humanity itself contributes to and sustains through its selfishness and ignorance, and herein it is contained through evil occult methodology and fear.

It is pertinent today to question what is this organised system of civilisation that humanity has intentionally been herded into and now accepts as a way of life?

Most of humanity today lives in a prescribed reality into which it has been seduced and then controlled by those of darkness, who over generations have used fear, deception and force to shift humanity into its present consciousness prison. This prison is sustained and up kept by humanity through its ignorance and self-maintenance, surrendering to and empowering an order of hierarchal rule which has sought to use them for its own ends in a compact with greater evil that has come to rule this planet. As many are presently awakening to the great and vast extent that such evil is being perpetrated upon the collective, they will realise that humanity has been collectively and psychically overthrown having surrendered to this involuntary group and adopted its version of illusory reality. This degenerated world, in its apathy, compliance and spiritual indifference has today prostrated itself before cosmic evil as its father and guide. This evil is expressing itself today as the new world order – an evil barely resisted or even acknowledged by most of humanity until today.

Quite literally in exchange for its true soul, humanity has adopted this involuntary way of life and pseudo-reality at the expense of all that is truly good. They have now become an integral part and play of cosmic evil which essentially uses them as batteries and pawns to serve its own ends within the cosmic scheme of life. This vast and seemingly complex illusion and glamour of civilisation is merely one great distraction and could soon ultimately bring upon humanity's self-destruction which today is becoming all too apparent to those who are looking out over the world and seeing the doom that is now inevitably approaching. This planetary destruction has always been within the greater plan of cosmic evil despite its vain and deceptive promises to its servants and keepers.

Humanity, though you may be seduced into the great

illusion of a magnificent social reality – aspiring to great wealth, fame and power – you may delude each other into thinking that your great trials, frustrations and pains that you suffer by keeping this dying yet thriving civilisation inspired and maintained, account for something greater and of importance. You may think that through serving the great yet redundant religions of the world, shrouding your hearts and minds with the great hypocrisies and lies that they tell you, that you will get closer to God. You may delude yourselves to think that today's society means something in the face of what looks like the total destruction of humanity, yet in the end you shall find that all these pseudo and hypocritical efforts are all born of self and shall come to naught. Civilisation today stands as merely one great vacuum and is highly estranged from that which is true.

This great tower of untruth that is called civilisation is but a great siphon of energy used by planetary evil to feed and sustain itself and the greater evil that they are subservient to. Together this group of planetary dark masters have, over time, shifted and inverted humanity almost in its totality and today stand under direct alignment in magnetic attraction to cosmic evil. This ring of masters is but an ethereal circuit and negative vortex that feeds off humanity's energy that acts as a gateway to a greater hell of psychic distortion. It is this group, in its magnetic attraction, that keeps humanity sustained within its negative field of involution and duality.

Civilisation today thrives on and through a negative synergetic attraction attempted through human personalities into a forced unification that is magnetically held by fear. It is through identification with its collective ego that Lucifer seduces humanity into estrangement from Christ. Today, most of humanity in its subversion into gross materialism and 'I' identification, has turned outward, misplacing their true birthright to adopt evil as its protector, guide, father and polarised anti-Christ do they fulfil that which has been prophesied throughout the ages. The new world order is a grand attempt at establishing the perfect society of hierarchal rule and evil in which those dark masters and ruling elite control the race through manipulation and falsehood. Few people can truly understand the colossal effort and energy spent to construct this grand orchestration of lies, illusion and inevitable futility, and humanity has some rather big and shocking surprises in store for itself!

All the truly aware of the Earth today look forward to the inevitable destruction of this great and unholy tower. Those who are taking leave of this fallen reality and walking in living faith are heralding within Christ's immanent and prophesied return in power, which shall soon throw those of unholy reign from their thrones. Momentarily driven by their great evil and fear to take this short stand against divine love, truth and will, they will now be forced and cast with all their lesser minions into the very abyss that they, themselves, have opened.

THE BROTHERS OF SHADOW

After the fall of Atlantis some of the more powerful sorcerers of darkness, sometimes known as the brothers of shadow, survived and scattered themselves throughout the planet. These sorcerers did this by binding themselves to certain places of power in order to recuperate their energies and preserve themselves.

Such power sites may in the past have been places of human sacrifice, magic and atrocity, many of which are still hidden and preserved today by the dark energies that protect them. From these points, these sorcerers over time began setting up their various lineages throughout the world. Each lineage itself being a tentacle for cosmic evil in its search for the recruitment of human beings on the planet.

Initiation into the dark brotherhood

These "brotherhoods" rely on deception and often ghastly induction methods to recruit candidates into their various lineages and collective, miscreant energies.

To understand the process of their more ancient initiation methodology, we are able, with insight, to see how cosmic evil is corrupting so many beings today globally.

The full intricacies of candidate selection and initiation are not known to this writer, who is sharing from relatively flawed personal experience and information. However, one can assume that over time each lineage has cultivated its own adaptation of induction, but on the whole the methodology is basically the same.

Potential recruits will be self-seeking beings wanting to experience paranormal and occult experiences, usually with some motivating selfish undertone of empowerment, material wealth and even personal enlightenment, etc.

The more evidently darker lineages, however, seek strong-willed candidates who can withstand the terrors, dangers and tensions of induction. After choosing a candidate, one of the brothers (in one such lineage calling himself a 'brujo') makes contact either personally in the physical world and/or psychically.

Using a candidate's intrigue against himself, the sorcerer can psychically seduce the candidate to pursue him while remaining aloof and distant. Subtly enticing with promises of power and knowledge, the candidate is left to pursue their offering, motivated by the candidate's self-will, thus becoming an aspirant to the sorcerer's cause. The sorcerer may then begin to instruct the candidate, presenting a "path" using such phrases as "warriorship" and "the way", and initiate the aspirant into becoming a "seeker" of knowledge and power.

To compliment this they encourage their students with words of superficial or inverted wisdom, and may even include utterances of "love and light", which are difficult if not impossible for the student to comprehend. In this way they entice the student to strain mentally to attain such aloof concepts, thereby drawing them further into personal desire and the resulting vulnerability to illusion, deception and manipulation.

Then over a period of sometimes years they can withdraw their students somewhat from society. Some teachers then begin to acquaint them with various psychotropic concoctions using advanced pharmaceuticals, chemical agents or special plant based hallucinogens. (I have even seen beneficial medicinal plants such as Ayahuasca or Datura held hostage and mixed with various other plants to suit a sorcerer's agenda.)

In such induced states of mental and psychic displacement, the powers of darkness are able to manipulate the consciousness of their apprentices and induce states of illusion, producing paranormal experiences. Having withdrawn their candidates from society, which enables greater control, they can then work through paranoia and uncertainty to cultivate attachment, fear and confusion.

Throughout this relationship the teacher seduces his student to believe that to become a man of power he must first learn to "see". This "seeing" is an abstract concept and a "reward" that works like a carrot dangling in front of a donkey to make it keep walking.

He also relates to the student that "seeing" is only accomplished by strict obedience to "the way", which is but a psychological constriction and directive. He tells the student that it is a way fraught with danger but subtly assures him that, as a teacher, he is able to give safe passage.

While darker lineages do not hide their evil intent, some use terms such as "warrior", "seeker" and "the way". The aspirant is lured, through self-deception, to believe that he is going about some noble cause, hence feeding his ego and giving him great determination through self-will to battle on.

The student may be given a series of complimentary exercises, mantras, spells and body stances in which the shadow forces can then transmit their peculiar energies to the recipient that provide the teacher-sorcerer with even greater access and control.

Together with the continual and sporadic use of their psychotropic concoctions these exercises are used to induce extreme psychological states, creating such mental distortion and confusion to facilitate the brothers of shadow to directly implant seeds of fear and produce severe hallucinogenic experiences.

Some examples of such exercises are:
* Running through the jungle blindfolded, while being pursued by an unknown evil entity.
* Staring at a shadow fixedly until they can see.
* Being alone in a dark room and walking or rolling around the floor until a "place of power" is found.

The aspirant who is inspired through his dedication to "warriorship" often forces himself to stand and stare for days, to the brink of exhaustion. Then, when he is in such a state of psychological turmoil that he is hallucinating or has collapsed, in walks the teacher and rewards him with affirmations such as: "Now you are beginning to see" or "you've found your place of power!"

Now seeing that his student is willing to go to such extremes and is under his influence, the sorcerer then introduces the student to another "brujo" in which together they set upon further manipulation – one taking the role of guide and teacher, the other playing upon the student's terror and exhaustion.

During a process of psychic manipulation known only to them, they then proceed to work upon and slowly cleave the mind's reasoning faculty from its creative side.

Such polarity and separation rends the student's protective, psychic web and enables the forces of evil to directly infiltrate and take control.

This also gives the sorcerers complete access and

then it is possible for them to directly implant certain psychic attributes in the consciousness of the student so that he may perform feats such as levitation, teleportation and the like.

Their student, now completely open and vulnerable to auric manipulation, can then readily have experiences such as astral travelling, remote viewing, even shape shifting (which such 'brujos' are renown for).

By forcing their students into such unnatural states far removed from practical sanity, the sorcerers increase their personal power – power that has been fed through the development of psychic abilities over time through these dark lineages – often posing as light, they create severe psychological abstraction.

From such states, aspirants and sorcerers have gained a twisted insight into things, but really it is an "outsight", an inverted knowledge from which they are able to "see" humanity and the world from completely unnatural perspectives. Thus the term "seeing" is relative and is at the unimaginable cost of the spiritual, mental and psychic stability of the student. What the aspirant does not "see" is that they are slowly beginning a process of inverting their entire auric field and consciousness!

Slowly and over time they open themselves to foreign manipulation, grafting certain inimical implants by which they feed the unnatural energies that lie behind the various dark lineages. Unknown to them they are then in the perfidious grip and are participating in a hierarchy of intelligent evil.

As their consciousness dwells within such points of abstraction they are even able to see human and planetary energy fields in a perverted way, and over generations have, as recruited disciples, learned through tried and tested methods to slowly gain a twisted mastery of manipulation with regard to humanity. These beings are able to shut down humanity's chakras, manipulate auric fields and leech off planetary energy grids.

The partial inversion and infiltration of their auric field requires them to vampirise humankind for energy in order to sustain their personal life force. They are therefore coerced to become more parasitic in their career as they are led by their teachers into further abstraction requiring them to seek students themselves to secure their own sustenance and that of their group. In the earlier stages and unknown to them they have become agents of cosmic evil, which they have been (sometimes for millennia) assisting such evil in what on a grander scale is a plan for planetary induction.

What the student often does not know is that their teachers have not been recruiting individually and that the sorcerer usually has a group of students he has been working with simultaneously yet independently. Later the teacher-sorcerer brings together all his "successful" students so that they may collectively go through a series of group initiations.

I have felt it necessary to release such information, though it is somewhat coarse and flawed. (Such lineages protect their secrets). It is based on more ancient techniques used to try to manipulate and recruit me by a sorcerer in my younger years which was followed by a series of black magic attacks that lasted many months as I worked out their manipulation. "Their Way" is founded upon the inversion of true divine initiation.

Looking around the world today one can see some interesting parallels of such induction on a global scale, not only in the psychic and pseudo-spiritual arena but also in religion, politics, media, education, the military, etc.

What we can see being revealed is more modern and scientific methods of induction using social engineering, propaganda through the media and MK –ultra techniques.

These represent tentacles of cosmic evil, which are present and working within many worlds and dimensions, slowly infiltrating, manipulating and ultimately consuming them.

As the world today plunges into further manipulated abstraction and distortion, we can see that humanity – individually and collectively – has been seduced into aligning itself with such evil, as it is drawn into an involute vortex of blindly active participation in its intelligence, while opening itself more and more to its miscreant energies and powers.

One can draw many parallels. For example, much

– even most – of the New Age movement, through its self-seeking and ignorance, is unconsciously assisting the plan of the planetary takeover. As people collectively strive to gain self-empowerment and personal enlightenment, applying themselves to practices of self-cultivation with certain "yogic techniques", they are in fact essentially not so different from those misguided individuals who stand for days on end staring into shadows: the ultimate effects are the same.

The forces of darkness thoroughly understand the dualistic processes of humanity's individual and collective mind, and they have worked assiduously for ages to subtly increase states of tension and planetary confusion, while inducing great struggles within dualistic polarity. Television is today a primary tool of collective exploitation. This renders open the protective, psychic web of mankind on Earth, in which cosmic evil can then infiltrate directly with very little resistance.

Over time and through its countless agents, conscious or unconscious, the plan of cosmic evil has developed and cultivated innumerable groups and sub-groups within human consciousness and activity to such a degree of abstraction that by way of their essentially self-serving intentions, that they are creating technologies, manipulating planetary energy fields and ultimately seeding their own self-destruction.

Humanity has thus been methodically withdrawn from the greater Cosmos. Now many of these unfortunate beings have been individually and collectively exposed, implanted and grafted. They are becoming an integral part of cosmic evil,—which is essentially instinctual, mechanical and utterly immoral.

In order to infiltrate whole planetary systems such as Earth's, evil uses human personalities produced by the planet as it rapes, steals and plunders humanity's consciousness to further its own twisted plan, to feed its own consciousness and to gain its "outsight" so that it may proceed with its plan of planetary control, consumption and destruction.

(This article, written at age 26, has been given minor adjustments.)

THE GOD OF ILLUSIONS

Most of humanity looks out into the created universe today and imagines an omnipotent god controlling and governing the known universe. Those somewhat more spiritually inclined offer adulations and praise to this almighty creator and seek consolation when their lives are troubled or their understandings perplexed. Few seek the very foundations upon which they make their offerings from nor do they question the apparent chaos and disharmony that engulf them continually upon their short and somewhat miserable journey through this existence.

It is seen that humanity assumes much and yet knows very little as to the nature of its existence and its surrounding reality!

When people talk about God, do not they usually seek to understand a god of their own aspirations?

Is it not a reflection of certain qualities of their very selves, their hopes and desires that they project upon what God is?

The Christian church fathers tell us to place all

our trust in God and tell us that their god is all loving, all-powerful and all-knowing, and they, as servants of God, offer themselves to this almighty creator upon the foundations that their spiritual forefathers have stood.

Affirmed in their belief and worship by the mighty words of the avatars and saints that have appeared throughout humanity's collective history they have interpreted and attributed most of the given qualities to their god which they have learned through the guidance of the church and which the church itself has cultivated and reinforced over successive millennia.

So great are these attributes and so fervent in their belief they are that their followers simply do not question such a grand orchestration and authority. And over those successive generations they have worshipped such an image that it has become part embedded within their very blood consciousness. As many have given their devotion, time and even their lives to appease their god, in the church, today 'faith' is merely instinctual and their 'belief' automatic as it has become absorbed deeply within their racial consciousness.

Should we look back through humanity's collective history, its energetic investment in god over countless lifetimes is massive. Great battles have been fought in 'god's name' with conquests and conversions galore!

Countless martyrs have offered their own little lives to this great unknowable that somehow the church fathers seem to know all too well.

But what is it that humanity truly serves?

What happens when a people surrender their hearts and minds to such images as they personally and collectively continue to affirm their own ideals and beliefs to their very selves and each other?

Then, through their maintained convictions dedicate their lives to that which they have been told, hope and even demand exists? Do they not through their own devices create a god in their own image?

Have they not projected and imposed their own will upon Truth?

And what of the strength of such an image when it has been cultivated over generations?

Can such a generated entity eventually dominate and overtake people's minds and hearts if they themselves exchange such falsehood over that which they innately sense is true and real – becoming the ignorant victims to such a reflected impression that is governed and manipulated by an outside authority?

It is time that humanity understands what they serve and perhaps voice aloud those unutterable words that fear and self-deception fight against. Those words that will not be uttered by those who bare false witness to truth!

That we, of ourselves, know nothing!

Let us not be afraid to see that mostly the foundations of human worship to 'God' are illusory and even cancerous in their effect and to put it simply: Most of your spiritual leaders, priests and gurus have been self-deceived and they have been lying to you!

Here it must be said that with these words we do not want to stir or inflame passions against such personages. Such beings would not even hold any such positions of authority if the collective itself would not give them the energy to fortify themselves in their illusions and let it be seen that many such leaders are quite pure in their intent as they mostly believe with a conviction in what they teach and say.

The root of their lie exists not only within their minds but within their hearts, and there it is fostered and reinforced every time they act discordantly with the truth of their hearts and deny their true soul to serve the outward principles and values of their illusory authority.

When most people speak of god in a personal way they are prescribing attributes and terms as defined by their own relative perceptions, conceptions and experiences of life. An ego centred consciousness ascribes its reality in terms of personal understanding and relativity.

To an awakening or awakened heart and consciousness, the ego may be understood or known as the centre of fear, or the 'I' consciousness.

It is a disassociated aspect of our original and full consciousness that perhaps one could say is the microcosmic product of an aspect of our greater cosmic consciousness that fell beyond the relative measures of what humanity terms as time and space.

As a disassociated aspect of our original and full consciousness it perverts into a perception that draws itself deeper into its own version of a distorted and twisted reality.

As most of humanity draws its understanding and knowledge through individual perception and relativity, it is not wrong to say that most people today are almost completely egocentric.

An egocentric consciousness is a limitation!

In fact, if it is strengthened and cultivated it can become a prison capturing a being in its own and partial version of temporal reality disconnecting them from higher aspects of reality. When it has become a fundamental basis and identification of a being's existence, they have effectively shut themselves off from true reality and have fundamentally rendered themselves from life.

Such a rupture with the true centre of being is a death as darkness envelops the heart and fear is the result. From a more spiritualised perspective one could quite understandably term such a vehicle as the walking dead.

One could also describe those whose dominant facet of existence is living through and as an ego as those who are living in fear.

When someone has died in such a said manner all that they truly have is an illusion of life and thus it is not strange when one begins to awaken from their relative darkness that they cry out that all life is an illusion!

An illusion is a projection of fear, and in a personal sense it is an image drawn from one's heart and mind to protect an ego from seeing the truth that is founded within the true centre of our being.

Those who live their lives purely egocentrically, live in and as an illusion. The ego itself cannot truly know anything but simply struggles to maintain and keep its existence thriving.

One of the curious survival impulses of a human ego is that it sees what it wants to see, hears only what it wants to hear and acts accordingly to what pleases and feeds it.

It mostly denies that which threatens its own interpretation of its illusory reality, thus its nature is averse to Divine Truth which it instinctually recognises as its enemy.

As a common defence a personality usually ascribes truth to itself and defends itself quite fiercely when it has been strongly cultivated and reinforced.

Turned outwardly into the phenomenal world, an ego asserts itself into identification with matter to affirm its reality and deny any inner impulse or call that might resound from Spirit!

Thus almost every impulse or desire that an egocentric and dominated consciousness acts upon or motivates is therefore usually in opposition to spiritual motive or awakening, and any truth, conception or ideal that it grasps upon of true divine reality is twisted, interpreted and reduced to its own personal perspective.

When such beings look out into phenomenal existence and surrender – attributing everything to their "God out there" – they have come to deny all that is truly real.

Having prostrated themselves before their god which is their inspired source of all their hopes, dreams and adulations, it is in truth their own individual and collective projection and reflection of fear. Such is humanity's great god of illusion!

Now when a divine personage appears or awakens upon the planet a great amount of true divine light and energy is radiated. At pertinent times in humanity's collective history the great ones such as Jesus, Gautama, Krishna and Mohammed have appeared as instruments of divinity to liberate those trapped divine sparks from their earthly prison. Well after they have departed from this world their resounding note and influence serves thousands of years afterward as a source of aspiration, inspiration and nourishment for entire civilizations.

Truly as one observes today's grand orchestration of religious institutions and cultural perspectives, one could say that such beings have made a great impression!

The light and impact such a being brings to the collective is painful, burning through the layers of Maya, glamour and illusion that the planetary ego waxes around itself. While blazing a path through such density and darkness it stimulates, awakens and releases many divine sparks from their prison but it also provokes, disturbs and burns the planetary ego that often and usually reacts with great pain and distress seeking to muffle, restrain and even destroy such an intruder that it sees as the cause of its pain and becomes their adversary.

It is thus why all the great ones have faced such formidable trials, obstacles and much suffering in their service and dispensation of light and truth.

After such a divine personage has served their mission of true salvation and departed, the planetary ego instinctually moves to re-assert itself and is relatively swift and cunning in its response.

After a great one's departure the powerful and higher residual vibration and impression that such a being leaves upon the planet dynamically affects and impacts upon the remaining collective.

But such an impression must not be confused with the original and true divine salvific impulse which is received via the divine spark that lies at the true centre of one's being, which is the catharsis for true awakening and enlightenment.

It is but the 'bright shadow' that draws, affects and stirs the planetary ego in which it immediately seeks to utilise, to strengthen and reinforce itself! It is this false light that the planetary ego feeds and draws upon to maintain its illusory existence and empower its own twisted agenda.

Upon such higher impulses, energies and vibrations that such a divine being leaves in its wake the world ego creates its own interpretations and images of divine reality, truth and god to pervert, seduce and overpower those of true humanity into wrongful identification.

It does this to draw and feed off their essence and projections to maintain its own illusion!

This is the greatly guarded secret and foundation that mainstream religion today refuses to admit as they are the keepers of the great illusion. That these unholy imitators of divine truth and life are merely serving to keep and maintain a shadow!

When we look out over the world today this is what we see.

A more awakened being shudders at the great delusions of mankind.

Cultivated over millennia, mainstream and organised religion is but a sickening parody far removed from the original salvific impulses and teachings that originally initiated them. Using the images of the great ones, the planetary ego has created many false gods.

Prostrating themselves before these degenerating images their keepers and their followers only serve to keep humanity locked in their earthly prison as they successfully dominate and control the planetary consciousness.

The great confusion and distortion of the true teachings from the great ones under mainstream and organised religion from the passing age is today but a great dragnet upon the collective.

Their followers blind and deaf, clinging to images that lead astray, confuse and dominate many beings who are awakening to the new salvific impulse of the day!

They are lost in the refuse of the passing age and lack the innate ability, humility and honesty in the face of change as this world is put under increasing stimulation in accordance to divine decree.

As these cosmic rays of divine love and dissolution increase in their intensity formidable pressure is now to be continually exerted upon humanity.

Should humanity choose to remain fixed and unrepentant in its illusions, idealisms and ways they will suffer greatly by their own hands.

This has been forewarned by the various prophets, seers and divine beings throughout humanity's collective history, in which some have termed this tumultuous phase of great change Armageddon.

Those religious figures and keepers who continue to impose their evil authority and dominance upon the collective shall now be forcefully and finally thrown from their seats of power.

The glory and truth of the coming age has been greatly dimmed and distorted by those who would suffer others to their delusions, deceptions and self-gratifications.

Now in this final stage of the planetary corrective

process those beings who refuse to align and submit to divine will and decree shall now be removed from this world as she awakens and moves on to her rightful place.

FALSE OFFERINGS

Groups, organisations and people serving Life are only purposeful when they are acting in true response to the incoming light and revelation of the world soul. Truth, though ever immutable and unchangeable, is responded to accordingly through the variable conditions of fallen life and thus subject to change within the fluctuating conditions of response within the collective's outer dualistic mind. Thus, that which humanity finds truthful and purposeful today, becomes falsehood tomorrow. Those teachings that yesterday helped liberate the collective today turns to imprison it. The shifting sands of the outer conditions of earthly life change throughout its history as do the very winds that blow upon the Earth's surface.

At present there are many motivated individuals and groups, who, along the lines of earthly service, have falsely labelled, associated and even considered themselves to be the spiritual benefactors of humanity. Applying all and various, means and ideologies, to improve or save the planet via their own limited and personal views of truth, righteousness and what is good for the world. So idealistically and actively fixated upon the so-called good that they believe that they are doing, the call to new life is passing them by.

In natural worldly response, incarnated servers will always apply humanitarian standards of conscience within their earthly field of service. Such earthly goodwill is the sympathetic action of an open and loving heart to those base needs and requirements of existence in material life. However, such earthly service itself is not a means to an end.

Today many are caught or lost in the blindness and inertia of previous and truly unrealised spiritual teachings and outmoded impulses of yesterday, and are unable to intelligently or dynamically respond to the call of truth as it resounds within the present. The outer courts of this world are littered with such groups offering false hope, idealistic truths and redundant teachings that miserably fail in bringing divine Love to Earth.

Few today are able or even willing to truly empty and still themselves, allowing the reorientation processes of divine Life to take them in hand and guide them as to what is truly needed to effectively bring about those necessary changes within earthly life and truly prepare as the great transition now speeds up hastily upon the outer planes of existence. Full of self, blind and unheeding do such beings chase their own tails within this labyrinth of dualistic life. For even with the best yet ignorant intentions such earthly or redundant offerings in effect are now truly denying that which is truly good and are doing great disservice to all.

There are many groups and individuals that lack true divine contact or experience, feigning light through false mystical occult practices and dualistic activities – purposely leading astray the masses to suit their own intentions or fallen perspectives of truth – misguiding and confusing many while outwardly making displays of their service in false praise to God. These are the tenors of hypocrisy and behind them flourish the greater evils of the world. Verily, today, the call to New Life goes mostly unheeded and the counterfeit spirit abounds.

Followers of older teachings should realise that such teachings are but the outward expression of the indwelling Life. Mere acknowledgement, affirmation of outward principles and attempts of self-transcendence through imitation has turned such teachings into the great parody and unfortunate burden that now weighs heavily upon humanity's shoulders. Without sound and true divine realisation such followers of their outer tenants are leading the world into great misfortune, further complicating the illusive conditions of a fast deteriorating world. Such teachings harnessed by those self-motivated individuals and groups to further their own designs are now having a definite and truly awful result upon the misguided and immature collective.

The true inner nature of the disciple or initiate is the ever yearning, thirsting and seeking indwelling soul, realising the true nature of dualistic life, crying for release. In truth there is but one offering that is necessary that opens the true way of initiation yet the ego would twist and contort such simplicity into all sorts of distortions, aberrations and concessions. The true required sacrifice that is to be offered upon the altar of Love is self! The many claims of initiation from such beings, affirmed by mental sophistry and cool self-determination, now, will not stand under the increasing pressure that the true life brings.

There is much talk and literature of a second coming, the coming one, planetary ascension. Such outer expositions have been quite dramatically and aberrantly twisted by the planetary ego to suit its own idealistic ways. Now it grapples with that which lies beyond its own twisted understanding. Few understand that divine Love will not find its way into human hearts until its outer courts are cleared personally and collectively. Until humanity truly yields up its idealisms and glamour, emptying itself of the false, can divine Love find its way into the collective human heart. Love will not enter a den of thieves.

The great contortion of truth within the mind and heart of humanity has made it almost completely unresponsive to the new call of Spirit today. Today love shall pass by the houses of many for none shall open the door. Yet now as the Sword of divine Truth enters this world such beings and groups shall be exposed for what they truly are. The heavy yoke that they have placed upon humanity shall now be lifted as they and their false offerings are delivered to the shadows of redundancy. The light of divine Truth shall reveal those who would counterfeit the spirit and reveal the corruption that has grown within the collective's heart.

For with all said and done today evil is outwardly and openly flourishing and thriving on Earth. Though symbols and words of love abound, such offerings are but the dualistic imposition of the perhaps well-meaning yet unenlightened. Declarations of love and light propelled by self-will, blind belief and conviction have in effect done nothing to truly arrest the growing evil upon the planet and are simply impotent in effect and meaningless in bringing the divine plan into true manifestation.

PSEUDO OCCULTISM

Today the dangers of pseudo-occultism are highlighted!

Those vain, deceitful yet popular teachings that are dispersed throughout bookstores, New Age/mystical outlets and internet forums are now being seen for what they truly are.

A measure of a true teacher can be given by one's students, and today one may observe a plethora of occult groups, "spiritual" communities and forums, and clearly see many sincere yet confused aspirants struggling with and against those beings who are psychotic, half-hearted in approach and sometimes even truly predatory in nature. Attracting all and various- let true doubt be cast upon those teachers and teachings who allow all and sundry to come under their feet.

Such beings cast dispersions, attack personalities and/or seduce those sincere yet immature aspirants into corrupted dualistic interplay.

Young and struggling seekers often become confused and distracted, and are usually compelled or psychically manipulated to engage in unknowingly serving and feeding the darkened host of the subtle realms through coercion and misplaced attention.

So-called teachers, group leaders, gurus and group moderators who allow those under their supervision and care to sow discontent and intentional confusion – or who allow peddling of the non-essential or the mis-informative – are in fact serving those darkened forces by enabling them to openly flower in their corruptive purposes.

Such leaders compromise their own serviceful intentions and understandings, and severely confuse and harm those who sincerely seek the New Life amidst the great spiritual egotism, misinformation and deceptive teachings that litter the so-called "spiritual supermarket" of today. Thus these teachers are karmically and energetically engaging and becoming entangled in what are truly unwholesome practices serving Lucifer and his host.

True group service in true alignment with the divine plan is virtually unknown and almost completely misunderstood within humanity today. The divine inner nature and synthesis of true group work in alignment with the divine plan is a far cry from those many and assorted groups who feebly labour in "God's name"!

True group service has nothing to do with surrendering oneself to mere idealism based upon teachings of those who expound seemingly higher occult knowledge!

Gatherings of such personalities are mere cults

pursuing self-service with no true divine contact or inspiration. Often seen amongst their followers or students is a blind adherence to their teacher or teachings. Lacking true discernment and openly prejudicial, they are not able to receive true divine assistance.

Thus, psychically trapping and energetically binding each other by generating their illusions and glamour within such group fields, these cults can become powerful obstacles to divine realisation as each member reinforces each other energetically and egoistically.

Today, capable aspirants are cautioned to be alert in these times of mass deception and confusion and urged to truly question their own motives and inner sincerity, should they seek to become of true service to the divine plan on Earth.

Know that those who seek outwardly common ground to serve their own shared idealism – be it world salvation, ascension and/or healing programs – without true innate divine realisation or guidance are at best blind fools, or worse still, servants of the great and growing darkness upon the Earth.

Verily the counterfeit spirit abounds!

What is apparent to those who can see and can understand is that what such pseudo-occult groups and teachings fail to radiate is a true divine field or vibration.

Without true divine realisation it is impossible to understand the true nature of events that are unfolding within the current Armageddon. As entering cosmic energies continue to affect all planetary life, many are gazing in apprehension as the growing wave of darkness rises over humanity and are unable to comprehend what is truly happening. Under cosmic impulse, growing reactional and dualistic conflicts are arising from within, and those who are caught within the illusion are now to feel the great and inevitable pressure of the incoming Will Energy!

Humanity's misguided aspirations and inherent misconceptions as to its true planetary situation have led it to its current and now inevitable crises that shall now have serious repercussions upon the outer planes of existence.

Naive spiritualists and occultists, in their ignorance and misunderstanding as to the true nature of such a planetary event, cling to their teachings, delusional dogmas and unfulfilled promises of world saviours that are coming to save the Earth.

It is evident that the true planetary hierarchy has failed to impress upon a self-indulgent and immature collective the true nature of initiation, and their teachings have been greatly twisted and adulterated by the planetary ego.

The teachings of Christ are being proclaimed by the hordes and truly the most twisted and blasphemous absurdities are being proclaimed!

Thus the sword is raised to those miscreant, deceitful and delusional labourers in the darkness of untruth for the guardians of the sacred do not stand by idly when such evil is so openly pronounced.

POSITIVELY CONFUSED!

It has often raised an eyebrow here that despite degenerating worldly conditions and escalating madness, there are still relatively few people who are willing to open their eyes to see or attempt to understand the true planetary situation.

Often, one has seen that when honest people are speaking truthfully and openly about the inherent suffering of the world or the evils being exposed within the human race, they are often accused of "negativity" or being "dark". Again, when there is genuine discussion of the impending changes, problems or possible tribulations which we are all facing today, most people seem to close up or turn away. There are others who when overhearing talk about those manipulative forces that have seized control of the planet, consider it "evil" or a "conspiracy theory" to speak about such things.

There must be a definite understanding as to what is meant here. One here is not saying we should dwell upon those shadows of Earth or lose oneself to morbidity; this would lead only to depression and sickness. It is more the impulse of avoidance and deep mainstream denial of what is transpiring on our planet and what is truly happening within the collective that this piece is written for.

Let's get straight to the point.
Since when has "spirituality" and "positivity" come at the expense of truth?
Today there is so much talk about "being positive", looking at the good side of things and avoiding the "bad". In western society, and particularly in the New Age movement, this associative exclusion has resulted in a lot of very superficial "spiritual" dogma and cognitive dissonance. The lack of depth and misguidance of such people is obvious and can make true seekers cringe because today they see a growing madness in the eyes of those who sound their various rallying cries such as; "we are all One" and "save the world".

Today, these emotive impulses have been easily manipulated and played upon by various entities who know where humanity's reactionary instincts spawn from. They understand humanity's many delusions about the nature of reality, which is based mostly on propagated fantasies and self-deceptions. Feeding people false narratives through the media, they have been using such groups to achieve their goal of planetary usurpation.

Under the increasing pressure of our planetary catharsis, many such "pro-active positivists" will find it harder to keep their positive expectations and perceptions thriving in the face of escalating world tension, confusion and changing relativities. In fact many will be unable to avoid swinging into their polar opposite which is depression, submission and even madness as the tempo of life is raised and certain truths become revealed. All this is because too few come to truly understand the true nature of themselves and the reality which they find themselves in.

So from where does all this confusion arise?

The Blessed one said... *It is because the ignorant cling to names, signs and ideas; as their minds move along these channels they feed on multiplicities of objects and fall into the notion of an ego-soul and what belongs to it; they make discriminations of good and bad among appearances and cling to the agreeable. As they thus cling there is a reversion to ignorance, and karma born of greed, anger and folly is accumulated. As the accumulation of karma goes on they become imprisoned in a cocoon of discrimination and are thenceforth unable to free themselves from the round of birth and death. (The Lankavatara Sutra – Buddha)*

Whenever we turn outside and cling to the illusory reality we fall deeper from what is real. We lose our true connectivity to divine Life and perceive ourselves separate from our true essential unity. Think of wayward humanity...in almost all our actions, thoughts and words we are constantly affirming and reinforcing our prison.

And what is that prison?

It is the self, the personality!

It is the personality-identified being that is the prison and all the energies in which our fallen microcosm thrives. Its extension includes the collective world ego and all those forces and intelligences that we as personalities resonate with.

This has all come about through a fallen relativity.

As we cast our world-weary eyes across our vast and sprawling civilisation, we see a lost humanity revelling in its own self-centred illusions. In fact the New Age has seemed to make a religion out of it!
    Self, self, self...that is today's New Age religion!

Self-help, self-healing, self-enlightenment...the list goes on and on...all disguised as spiritual awakening!

Thus, that which keeps and feeds the personality-self is seen as positive while all that is deemed a threat to our self-perceived realities is negative, bad or evil. That which affirms our world of relativities and keeps humanity thriving in its illusions is good while those who expose humanity's inherent sufferings and deceits are labelled negative or dark.

This is because in a world that revels in falsehood such people bring with them the deep pain of realisation – despite what we want this world to be, or if we believe that we can make it better – that it will always fall way short of the mark. That in our superficial and misaligned attempts to make this world an order that is acceptable to ourselves and God, we can only sink deeper into hell and suffering.

So as one looks a little deeper, what are so many new agers and "positivists" fearing?

It is Divine Truth!

This is the true anathema to this wayward world as it thrives in its illusions. This is the "great enemy" that the world ego is subconsciously arming itself against. For the living Truth is the destroyer of self and its ways.

It is the unknowable, the ungraspable, the great "darkness" which the world ego and its keepers are today waging its war against. Consuming themselves in their great fear as the new energies bring with them those divine intelligences and servers that threaten to undo them all!

Have you ever wondered why all True spiritual beings have been attacked, mistreated and scorned?

In this involute world people fear to let go of their illusions. They bury their heads in the sand and cannot let go of their small and petty worlds of relativity. In today's rising world confusion and tension much of humanity is retreating deeper into self, thrusting themselves into mundane work, trivial pursuits and selfish entertainment.

People are even using "spirituality", "truth seeking" and "world service" to perpetuate the lie!

If they would be honest, they would see that all they are really doing is merely "self-service" and are falling even deeper into the illusion no matter how well disguised their true intentions are from themselves and each other.

To see the suffering, evils and wrongs of this world equates to failure for such people and mostly their denial protects them from exposing their deep inner wound.

It is easy to observe today that many new agers

seek to use "God", "Truth" and "Spirituality" to feed or distract themselves.

Their displays of goodness and spirituality are often just ways of obtaining self-verification and affirmation using displays of "goodness" and "Love and Light" to achieve this end. By immersing themselves into the drama of existence they avoid the essential schism and dawning truth that everything that is generated and perpetuated by the separative self only reinforces our collective prison. Their false "Love and Light" is one of the fundamental delusions that is keeping themselves and the world in wrongful identification and perpetual suffering!

In their continual affirmation of this grand play and illusion, humanity reinforces this archonic matrix reality by giving it substance and power over themselves.

Everyone is looking in the wrong direction.

Know there is no salvation "out there"!

The multitudes were wild with selfish thought; none recognised the rights and needs of any other one. The stronger pushed the weak aside, and trampled on them in their haste to be the first to get a blessing for himself. And Jesus said, Behold the cage of beasts untamed; a den of stinging vipers, maddened by their fiendish greed of selfish gain! I

Warren Sunkar

tell you, men, the benefits that come to men who see no further than themselves are baubles in the morning light; They are unreal; they pass away. (The Aquarian Gospel of Jesus the Christ)

"THE NEW AGE"
When "Waking Up" just means deeper sleep!

We would also like to make clear that although you may consider this manual a "New Age" publication, we do not. That is because what you are calling "New Age" is just the final manifestation of the old age. ZOEV JHO, ET 101

New agers, truth seekers, light workers...over the decades people have heard many such names and labels from those who have received much self-satisfaction in attributing themselves to be the benefactors and gurus of the global awakening that is taking place within this crucial hour of humanity's transition. Yet as one looks out over the vast sea of struggling, confused and often psychotic assortment of personalities claiming enlightenment, truth and divinity, it only seems here to stir the prolonged pain and realisation of how the glamour of deep self-delusion is still today keeping so many from accessing true divine potentiality.

What has become clear in this hour is that many so-called spiritualists and new agers highlight today's raging psychoses of a people struggling to deny the truth of the true planetary situation in which they find themselves. This article does not seek to frighten people or cast dispersions but to indicate that in the face of what is now coming, those with a deep investment in the Maya of this world – or those who find themselves immersed or clinging to such glamour and illusion – will only find great confusion, fear and possibly madness as today's realities swiftly change and they realise they are not in true alignment with the great divine cause.

In fact many will soon have the sad realisation that they have been working in opposition to it despite their "good and positive intentions"!

Again, let us get straight to the point.

YOU are not "spiritual" because you play with crystals, do yoga, are psychic, heal with reiki or massage, eat organic food, use essential oils.

YOU are not "awakened" because you surround yourself with like-minded people who parrot "Love and Light", "We are all one", "There is no evil", "I am a spiritual being having a human experience" etc.

YOU cannot "save the world" nor were you ever meant to!

In fact to use the words "Spirit or Awakened" in connection with any of these pursuits, therapies and delusions is mostly a gross misrepresentation of Truth and only serves to hijack or counterfeit the true work that is being done today by those servers of the race in true and right alignment.

Beliefs are just illusions and will only serve a purpose if they lead people to the realisation of Truth. As a platform for one's "reality" they are simply fictional or evanescent, and only indicate a lack of inner knowing or true gnosis. To base one's life on mere beliefs and projections, will only in today's changing social and spiritual climate lead to psychological disaster as people will find it very hard to reconcile their own "versions of reality" with the Truth that now emerges.

Your personal self is a construct – its belief structures, personal perceptions and intellectualisations are merely phantoms of Truth. They are constantly fed and maintained by those yet to find and stabilise in true divine alignment.

As the new energies pour into this world and the planetary ego fractures, know that such personal and collective constructs will completely collapse as things start to intensify.

For these new energies are ones of dissolution, and at the end of an age it is not about thriving in and adding more delusion to personality life but completely the opposite. It is about learning to release to the real and die to all self-definitions!

Be clear – we are not talking about physical death but true esoteric death and rebirth.

Only as the false lights turn off does the real turn on!

True awakening comes about by truly ridding oneself of glamour and illusion, not by indulging in it. Humanity, open your real eyes and see things as they truly are. That mostly, your mantras of "Love and Light" and "Peace on Earth" are just gentle songs of the self, playing upon each other to keep you comfortable and asleep!

Fear and self-delusion come in many guises!

What most new agers and spiritualists understand as their so-called "higher self" is but an inverted response and reception to a finer and subjective aspect of their microcosm.

This "voice" is not divine but the "great deceiver" that today holds many such people in confusion and thrall!

While many "spiritualists and new agers" have received wake-up calls from the true Divine Soul they have failed to recognise their true significance. It should now be obvious to many that most who have assumed enlightenment or spiritual awakening – and under the influence of their "higher selves" – have called or thought themselves teachers and gurus and have written books on "The path", "The Truth" and "God". Inwardly and in their subtle vanity they have deluded themselves to thinking themselves special or authoritative. Little do they realise that these touches represent simply the beginning of a much deeper process which they have stopped or greatly delayed because they were too drunk on their own self perceived divinity!

So let us assist and clarify...

Despite what many of you BELIEVE you are not YET children of God (in the true esoteric sense).

Most of you are not expressing any true "divine beingness".

You have to turn within and seek much deeper.

For the most part... YOU are merely a struggling personality trying to perpetuate your reality in any way possible.

The "I" greatly deceives itself and often you are willing to use your contorted, relative and hybrid version of so-called "spirituality" to achieve its aims.

I'm sure many of you will be repulsed by these words and even resentful!

You still seek in your spiritual immaturity those self-affirming clouds of fluff to keep your ego safe, pampered and full. But that will not serve you in this moment...the question is, do you really want to wake up?

Today, humanity's "dream" is fast becoming the collective nightmare.

Many people are scared of facing the possibilities of what is being said here.

How very few of you truly understand that it is in facing fear wherein lies the deep unravelling that allows you to open to true divine potentiality.

If you are caught up in the swelling fear of the planetary ego you will miss the shared grace of the deeper moment.

For it has been said that God is no respecter of personalities.

In the Light of Sol

Today the new comes with the death of the old and today's angel comes with an almighty sword.

Let it slay you!

PRIMAL SHAME

Those who face themselves know what fear is. The personality, the fallen self, the ego has us look out into the world, hiding from our inner pain and fear. The personality and its world is *all fear* and incident with fear is shame.

Understand here that we are not talking about guilt that keeps us trapped in the illusion. Here we speak of shame as an aspect of realisation and a portal to transcendent possibility through the inward admission that we are not living in alignment with what we know is true and real.

There are many things that trigger shame. People feel the shame of ego every time they act against their conscience or are caught. They feel the shame of their stupidities and their unworthiness, the futility and failure of each human attempt to heal or help this Earth and each other. Yet, most people hide from their shame. They want to be in control, override their inner realisations because they know what is right...

But the Living Truth reveals how little we do know and how blind we are.

Unwilling to feel shame's fire, unwilling to admit our foolishness to ourselves or each other, we push on in our fear, our blindness and madness and the problems of the world only get worse.

Fear distorts, it amplifies our illusions and has us looking outside of ourselves.

Deep within ourselves, there is the "shame of the fallen soul".

Within our deeper being we feel the shame of the fall. It is a remembrance of our loss, the tear from our divine innocence, the fall of the soul into personality identification and a life deprived of *Love*. This is ascribed as a deep terror and anguish in our depths. In desperate fear we hide from God and cling to our realities and illusions, using them as filters and mechanisms of self-feeding. We use the Earth and others to hide from looking within, to keep us distracted from our unbearable pain – that we live in a world of illusions and shadows.

Even deeper is the "shame of the fallen monad".

The shame of the self over God...the arrogance of the rebellion. It is the universal shame of one enacted within us thinking that it is us who are in control. With the cosmic inversion came our disconnection from *Life*. The pain of this shame has us push forward in our denial and terror...we exert our self-will.

Who would admit that *we* are the fallen ones? We are terrified to look at this.

Yet the fact that our little lives are played out on this Earth bears testimony to our fall!

People like to look out, separating themselves from others, judging, pushing their opinions. People sit in churches, mosques and synagogues and judge the "condemned ones". People cling to their occult books and knowledge or hold prideful to their intellectualisms or New Age ideals.

But the simple truth is that we know nothing at all and that *Truth* will soon bring us to our knees...

We like to blame others. We can blame everything on the illuminati, and we can even curse God. We will use anything to stop us seeing the lies and shame around the core of our being. Its pain is unbearable, a fire that torments us day and night from within the deepest recesses of our being.

Great change is here, and God's Truth is now bearing down on Earth. It will burn us if we are unwilling to see this and open to it, if we are unable to let Divine light into our fearing hearts and expose the shame of our miserable and wretched existence. For we are the liars, thieves and murderers. Every day we participate in and affirm this matrix of death.

The horror of our existence is coming to light – we are in hell.

Thank God! Because it cannot continue...

Let it all go, let *Truth* dissolve and clear out our arrogance and delusions that keep us in our endless pain and separate from each other. The day of purification is at hand.

In the fires of our purgatory lie our redemption. It is time to give it all up!

Let us not look out and judge but let us open to receive God's grace, let it free us from our misery. This is the great purification....nothing is hidden and may it all be exposed!

We must not be afraid to expose our wounds, everyone has them. Let Love lift you high and return you to the seat of true *Life*.

For the pure at heart shame can be a portal; its fire reveals our self-torture in our refusal to look inside ourselves.

Lay exposed and you will know what true humility is. Then lift your countenance to God. Don't be afraid of the unveiling truth within; ask for God's forgiveness then surrender. Face your fears and allow yourself to know the shame of being human and you might just be surprised!

If you could just let go then instead of tormenting or repelling us we just might have a divine consummation.

Then shall the fire of God be known for its sweetness for only when we have allowed the dross to be burnt away and all that separates us dissolve, can we experience the true bliss of God. Then the living waters shall pour over us...

There we shall see the Truth – that we have often been foolish and ignorant children!

THE FIRE OF GOD'S LOVE

Everyone knows how they are living is wrong.

Selfishness, materialism, egotism thrive in our so-called modern culture. We parasitise off Mother Earth with no care to the damage we are doing! Everyone uses and abuses each other to keep themselves afloat. We subject our children to a miscreant society that enslaves their minds and poisons their hearts.

Our civilisation is sick – we are sick – and the symptoms go unheeded. We see the desecration of the sacred in almost everything we do. Our lives oblivious to the call to change.

Did you think this would be allowed to continue!

Powerful energies are now being released through our Earth. Today the Divine Spirit comes into manifestation and with it comes the burning of all that will not receive it.

Judgement is here!

One here does not speak of the blinded and fiery zeal of the misguided church evangelists and their congregations who shout condemnation, the foolishness of New Age thought or the projections of the so-called truth movement.

Despite the disbelief or the sarcasms of the unheeding or spiritually dead, the great change has now come and is still coming. Everyone will pass through these fires.

Divine imposition is an act of God's mercy. The flaming sword of Truth is being driven through to the core of our beings. The avatar comes when we are unwilling or incapable of changing, when we are pulling ourselves and each other into hell!

Now it is change or be changed!

People's worlds are falling apart. Their cherished belief systems and the lies they tell themselves are being revealed for what they are. Many are having past events in their lives resurface in their minds, most are feeling an unknown pressure, others are contracting in fear. Karmic processes are coming back at a remarkable pace. All are symptoms of these cosmic fires entering our Earth.

People are looking for others to blame. They cling to the religions, intellectualisms and sciences to evade the Truth. The fearful will try to scuttle like cockroaches under their rocks but all is in vain for their safe houses will be overturned. Their hiding places and darkness revealed in the light that bores its way downwards into the hearts of all of humankind.

You cannot stop what has come into this world...but you can embrace it!

The energies that are growing in intensity are the

fires of God's Love. With them comes our redemption.

The pure in heart shall greet Truth's fire. Let it bring to the surface all the filth, rubbish and stupidity of our foolish little lives. In the cosmic fire lies regeneration and our transformation, and with it comes the presence of God. For those who understand, "God's wrath" contains the sweetest Love and realisation.

It is time to let it all go, to let go of this way of life that creates deep suffering and the pain of an existence with no hope but spiritual death. The new is here!

The Divine Fire will keep growing in intensity, until we fall to our knees. Everything impure will burn and continue to burn. The horror of civilisation stands revealed! It shall now fall. Let us all fall to our knees.

For those with eyes to see, the remarkable is now being revealed, God is showing his hand. The great tempering is now, and soon, no one will be able to deny this! Soon everyone will face the truth and know where they stand.

God be praised! The great *change* is here!

AS THE CLOUDS BREAK

It is important for those who are on the ascension timeline to be very aware of where they put their attention and energy. Engaging in involute realities will only open oneself to energy loss, auric contamination and/or dis-ease. Today many of us are being called to quickly let go of those people, realities and situations that no longer align with our ascension processes.

Those who are holding divine alignment are today naturally and inherently being guided to those people and places that hold mutually resonant energy fields as part of a group programme. These ascending planetary hubs are in calibration with the new planetary grid and these conscious grid workers are positioned strategically around the planet.

True grid workers aid in the establishment of metaphysical portals upon certain vortexes of the Earth's grid network. They find themselves in those areas so that they can bring divine influence and healing to certain locales, aiding planetary changes and clearing Earth's meridians and lines. These islands of light serve as magnetic centres galvanising and distributing the new incoming cosmic energies. This is achieved via true soul groupings through their collective synergetic potency.

While it is *not* necessary for incarnated individuals from group souls to be in physical proximity to each other, in respect to much of the grid work being done today, this might be a necessity in terms of people removing themselves from entropic situations and a fast deteriorating society.

Placed in strategic positions around the globe, ascending individuals will find themselves part of a carefully coordinated group process that will bring them into true collaboration with the more powerful divine beings and energies now present for the cleansing and shifting of the planet.

True group is naturally self-organising, organic and receptive to the divine impulse that they are serving. As Earth's frequencies are raised, the more powerful synergetic potency of group work and alignment further quickens and intensifies the catalytic energies available to those who are processing through a group directive. To safely handle such energies, true divine impersonality and non-attachment are needed to avoid personality confusion, frictions and blowouts.

With these intensified energies, suppressed emotions, misaligned tendencies and obsessions can quickly surface resulting in psychotic episodes, physical sickness and trauma as well as a large variety of ascension symptoms that are galvanised by the higher frequencies as part of the planetary quickening. We must be conscious in our preparations to withstand this coming period of high intensive energies, doing the work of clearing and releasing as much as we can to accommodate this cathartic process.

As this world is being corrected, we are reaching a point of complete energetic divergence between those who are aligning with the new incoming divine energies and those who refuse to change, clinging to a fast dying paradigm.

To navigate this period we are called to live by our highest standards of integrity. People need to release fear and realise that it is the living moment to which we self-surrender, that is the portal for divine grace and intelligence. It is we who invoke divine cooperation and assistance through pure living and genuine response to the call of the living spirit.

As we go through the intensification of energy and planetary processes those people on ascending timelines might also encounter attacks from those who seek to manipulate and control humanity from their hidden spheres. These wayward beings are growing desperate in the face of their own exposure and transiting. However, servers will find they have the inner coordinates and assistance to deal with such attacks and should not give in to fear and despondency.

As the clouds break and the light pours in, humanity

is reawakening its multidimensional potential. We will be forced to witness our self-deceptions, illusions and madness and know the control mechanisms that have been put in place to subdue and control Earth's population. People are realising they have been manipulated from both overt and hidden quarters and that we have been programmed, implanted and poisoned. We servers are often abused and psychically attacked.

Yet through it all this heart trembles with such love and gratitude.

For those whose hearts are open and eyes are clear, these days offer tremendous grace and oppotunity. Now as my eyes scan the Earth, I see my greater cosmic family are fast emerging from this dystopic dream. Theirs has been an amazing, beautiful and at times tragic story who through perseverance, heart and resilience in their love for Earth and its humanity, have battled and struggled through the madness and delusions of a subdued and crippled world.

They of the emergent new race are recognising each other and will not be clouded or subdued like the generations before them. They know themselves as One with the great Christ.

These children of God are awakening upon the Earth and know nothing will stop them…

www.ingramcontent.com/pod-product-compliance
Lightning Source LLC
Chambersburg PA
CBHW070627300426
44113CB00010B/1690